ACTIVITIES
MUSIC

Written by
Kirsty Holmes

Genius Kid

Library of Congress Control Number:
2024952957

ISBN
978-1-952455-21-6 (library bound)
978-1-952455-77-3 (paperback)
978-1-952455-60-5 (epub)
978-1-952455-41-4 (hosted ebook)

Printed in the United States of America
Mankato, MN
092025

Written by:
Kirsty Holmes

Edited by:
Elise Carraway

Designed by:
Ker Ker Lee

American adaptation copyright © 2026 by North Star Editions, Mendota Heights, MN 55120. All rights reserved. No part of this book may be reproduced or utilized in any form or by any means without written permission from the publisher.

Music © 2024 BookLife Publishing
This edition is published by arrangement with BookLife Publishing

sales@northstareditions.com | 888-417-0195

All facts, statistics, web addresses and URLs in this book were verified as valid and accurate at time of writing. No responsibility for any changes to external websites or references can be accepted by either the author or publisher.

Photo Credits – Images courtesy of Shutterstock.com, unless otherwise stated.

Cover – gresei, New Africa, Master1305, Sony Herdiana, Aleksandr Kondratov, CHALERMPHON SRISANG, Andrew Glushchenko, doomu, Mindscape studio, Wesley C.D, YellowPaul. 2–3 – RemarkEliza, Pixel-Shot. 4–5 – pmphoto, Roman Samborskyi, StockPhotoDirectors, Kiselev Andrey Valerevich, Anton Vierietin. 6–7 – VaLiza, Arcady, Anton Havelaar, stockphoto-graf. 8–9 – Anton Vierietin, Svetla Ilieva, faestock. 10–11 – Ljupco Smokovski, Matthias G. Ziegler, Ntguilty. 12–13 – Ljupco Smokovski. 14–15 – Master1305, faestock, Pixel-Shot, ABO PHOTOGRAPHY. 16–17 – yurakrasil, Pixel-Shot, Sergey Mironov, Elisanth, LightField Studios, MANDY GODBEHEAR. 18–19 – Pixel-Shot, RemarkEliza, Boris Medvedev. 20–21 – MyImages - Micha, Smit, Chizhevskaya Ekaterina. 22–23 – NDanko, FS Stock, italianestro, silvano audisio, wallerichmercie, conzorb.

CONTENTS

Page 4	Music
Page 6	Key Words
Page 8	A History of Music
Page 12	The Orchestra
Page 14	Folk Music
Page 16	Popular Music
Page 18	Becoming a Musician
Page 20	Believe It or Not!
Page 22	Are You a Genius Kid?
Page 24	Glossary and Index

Words that look like <u>this</u> can be found in the glossary on page 24.

MUSIC

Music is part of everyone's lives. Music can spark feelings or make people want to dance! What kind of music do you enjoy?

Beautiful instruments?

Loud guitars?

Funky beats?

Music is made up of sounds. The sounds are organized into patterns. Music is a way to express feelings, tell stories, or bring people together.

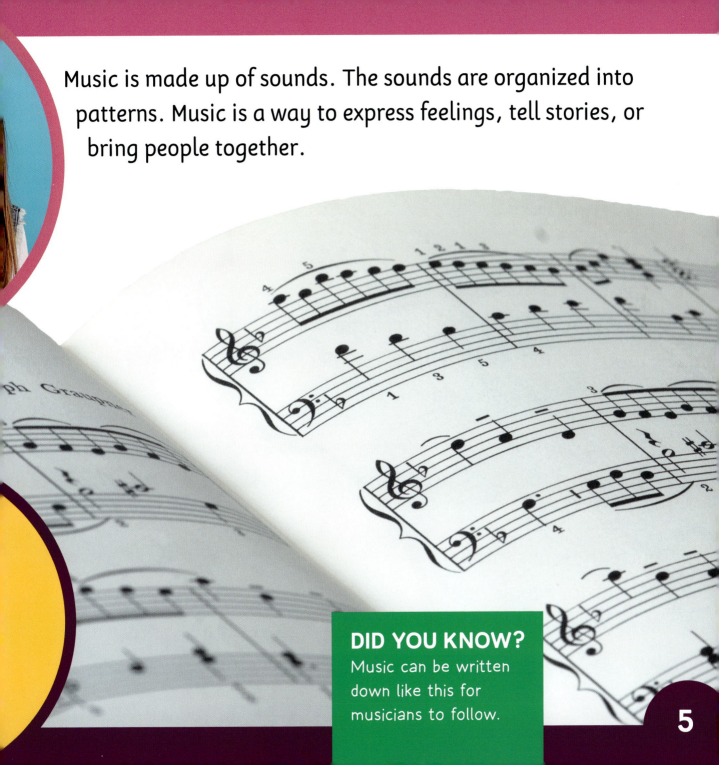

DID YOU KNOW?
Music can be written down like this for musicians to follow.

5

KEY WORDS

Here are some key words about music that every genius kid should learn.

MUSICAL NOTE
A musical note is a single sound. Many notes together make a melody.

Note

BEAT
The beat is a steady pulse that runs through the music. People can clap or tap along with it.

RHYTHM

A rhythm is a pattern of sounds and silences. Each sound can be a different length.

INSTRUMENTS

Instruments make sounds that we can put together to make a rhythm, a melody, or both!

A HISTORY OF MUSIC

Early Music, Around 5000 BCE
Early humans might have made music using sticks, stones, and animal bones.

The Middle Ages, 500–1500

People started to write down and share music for the first time. Music was also an important part of many religions.

We can see ancient Egyptian music in their art.

Ancient Egypt, Around 3000 BCE

Ancient Egyptians used music as part of important <u>ceremonies</u>.

Lyre

Western Classical Music, 1750–1820

Western classical music used big orchestras with many instruments. <u>Composers</u> included Mozart, Beethoven, and Bach.

Mozart

Jazz. From about 1900 onward
Jazz is fun and free. It was developed in the United States from African musical roots. Jazz musicians often improvise together. They make the music up as they play.

Popular Music. From the 1950s onward
Popular music is divided into groups called genres. Popular genres include rock, pop, metal, dance, and hip-hop.

Find out more about popular music on page 16.

11

THE ORCHESTRA

An orchestra is a large group of musicians. Orchestras play in a classical style. They are divided into different sections.

CONDUCTOR
The conductor uses a baton to guide the orchestra. The conductor keeps everyone playing together.

STRINGS
String instruments, such as violins and cellos, have strings or wires. You pluck them, strum them, or play them with a bow.

BRASS

Brass instruments are metal. You play them by buzzing your lips into a mouthpiece. Tubas and trombones are brass instruments.

WOODWIND

Woodwind instruments can be metal or wood. They include saxophones and clarinets.

PERCUSSION

Percussion instruments are played by being hit or shaken. Drums are percussion instruments.

13

FOLK MUSIC

Folk songs are an important part of many <u>cultures</u> and <u>communities</u>. Folk music tells the stories of the people. It is learned by listening to others.

Nursery rhymes and alphabet songs are folk songs for children.

Country music is based on American folk music.

In the Middle Ages, ballads were songs that told tales of heroic deeds.

DID YOU KNOW?
Most soccer teams have songs that all the fans know. These are a form of modern-day folk music.

15

POPULAR MUSIC

Popular music is music that lots of people like. Some popular genres are:

POP MUSIC
Pop music has catchy, boppy tunes and light-hearted lyrics.

DANCE MUSIC
Music made for dancing has a strong beat.

Heavy Metal

Punk

Rock 'n' Roll

ROCK MUSIC

Rock music uses guitars and drums. It is often loud and energetic. There are different types of rock music.

HIP-HOP

Hip-hop music uses rap over beats. It may also use <u>samples</u>. Hip-hop started in the United States in the Black community in the 1970s.

BECOMING A MUSICIAN

Anyone can make music. You do not need special instruments. All you need to do to master the art of music is practice, practice, practice!

CHOOSE YOUR INSTRUMENT
Which instrument will you choose—brass, string, woodwind, percussion, or voice?

TAKE SOME LESSONS
You could learn at school or pay for lessons from a music teacher.

PRACTICE MAKES PROGRESS
The more you practice, the better you will sound.

JAM TIME!
Playing music with others is so much fun. Can you join a choir, a band, or an orchestra?

BELIEVE IT OR NOT!

Music can affect the way plants grow. Apparently, plants grow best to classical and jazz music!

Birds use music too. Songbirds sing to defend their <u>territory</u> or attract a mate.

DID YOU KNOW?
Many songbirds learn their songs by listening to their parents. They imitate the tunes while still in the nest.

You might think a piano is a percussion instrument. After all, you hit the keys to play it. But a piano is also a string instrument! A piano has many strings inside it. When you press the keys, hammers hit these strings. This makes the sound.

ARE YOU A GENIUS KID?

Have you been making notes? It is time to get your brain tuned in—are you ready for the music quiz? Let's find out whether you really are a genius kid. And five, six, seven, eight … go!

Check back through the book if you are not sure.

1. What is the steady pulse that runs through music called?
2. What do we call things we use to make music?
3. What kind of music did Mozart compose?

Answers:
1. Beat, 2. Instruments, 3. Classical music.

GLOSSARY

ceremonies — actions that mark special occasions such as weddings
communities — groups of people living together
composers — people who write music
cultures — the traditions, ideas, and ways of life of groups of people
lyrics — the words to a song or a piece of music, usually sung
samples — small pieces of existing songs that someone else uses when making a new song
territory — the area where an animal lives and roams

INDEX

beats 4, 6, 16–17
composers 10
conductors 12
guitars 4, 17
instruments 4, 7, 10, 12–13, 18, 21

jazz 11, 20
orchestras 10, 12, 19
pianos 21
pop 11, 16
rock 11, 17